SCHOLASTIC

240 Vocabulary Words Kids Need to Know

Mela Ottaiano

New York • Toronto • London • Auckland • Sydney
Mexico City • New Delhi • Hong Kong • Buenos Aires

Cover design by Michelle H. Kim and Tannaz Fassihi
Interior design by Melinda Belter
Interior illustrations by Teresa Anderko, Maxie Chambliss,
Rusty Fletcher, James Graham Hale, and Sydney Wright

ISBN: 978-0-545-46051-4
First printing, May 2012.

17 18   40   23 22 21 20

Table of Contents

Using the Book

Where would we be without words? It's hard to imagine. Words are a basic building block of communication, and a strong vocabulary is an essential part of reading, writing, and speaking well. The purpose of this book is to help young learners expand the number of words they know and the ways in which they use them. Although 240 vocabulary words are introduced, many more words and meanings are woven into the book's 24 lessons.

Learning new words is not just about encountering them; it's about using, exploring, and thinking about them. So the lessons in this book are organized around different aspects and attributes of words—how words are formed using prefixes and suffixes, synonyms, antonyms, verbs, adjectives, homophones, homonyms, compound words, key content area vocabulary, and more.

Tips

- You'll find a complete alphabetized list of all the lesson words on page 78.

- As you introduce the lessons, have the following items available: beginning dictionaries and thesauruses, and writing notebooks or journals in which students can record words and use them in sentences.

LESSON ORGANIZATION

Each lesson includes three parts and introduces ten words.

The first lesson part includes:

The second part includes:

The third part includes:

lesson words

lesson words

lesson words

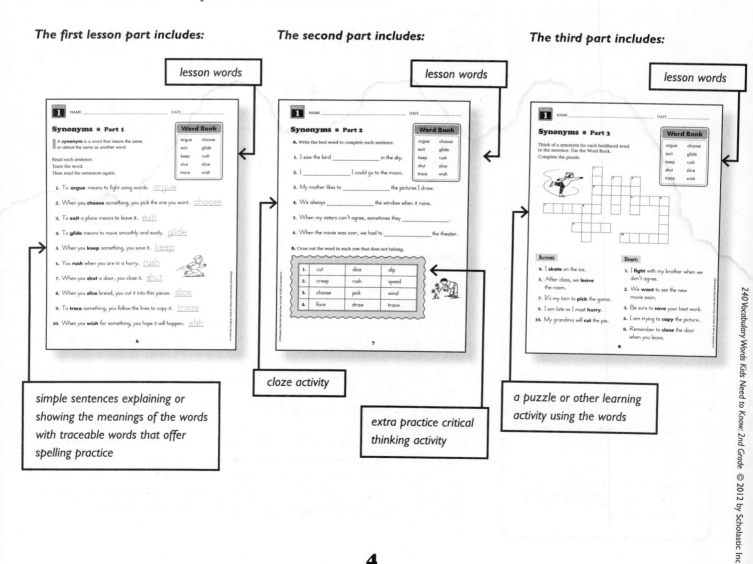

simple sentences explaining or showing the meanings of the words with traceable words that offer spelling practice

cloze activity

extra practice critical thinking activity

a puzzle or other learning activity using the words

240 Vocabulary Words Kids Need to Know: 2nd Grade © 2012 by Scholastic Inc.

Tips for Using the Lessons

- Consider having students fill out "Word Inventory Sheets" before each lesson. The headings for such a sheet might be: *Words I Know, Words I Have Seen but Don't Really Know; New Words.* Students can list the vocabulary words and probable meanings under the headings. As the lesson proceeds they can make revisions and additions.

- Each page in every three-part lesson uses all ten vocabulary words. The exercises on most of the pages use each vocabulary word once. Encourage students to think about the best word to complete a sentence or to answer each question.

- Some words have more than one meaning, including some not given in the lesson. You may want to point out additional meanings or invite students to discover them independently.

- Consider having students make a set of word cards for each lesson, or make a class set and place it in your writing center.

- Use the vocabulary to teach related spelling and grammar rules.

- Have students illustrate some words.

- Encourage students to make semantic maps for some words. For instance, they might create a map for a noun to show what the word is, and what it is like and not like.

- Help students make connections by pointing out lesson words used in other contexts and materials.

- Add your own writing assignments. The more students use a word, the more likely they are to "own" it.

Connections to the Common Core State Standards

The Common Core State Standards Initiative (CCSSI) has outlined learning expectations in English/Language Arts for students at different grade levels. The activities in this book align with the following standards for students in grade 2.

READING STANDARDS: FOUNDATIONAL SKILLS
Phonics and Word Recognition

3. Know and apply grade-level phonics and word analysis skills in decoding works.
   a. Distinguish long and short vowels when reading regularly spelled one-syllable words.
   b. Know spelling-sound correspondences for additional common vowel teams.
   c. Decode regularly spelled two-syllable words with long vowels.
   d. Decode words with common prefixes and suffixes.
   e. Identify words with inconsistent but common spelling-sound correspondences.
   f. Recognize and read grade-appropriate irregularly spelled words.

Fluency

4. Read with sufficient accuracy and fluency to support comprehension.
   c. Use context to confirm or self-correct word recognition and understanding, rereading as necessary.

LANGUAGE STANDARDS
Conventions of Standard English

1. Demonstrate command of the conventions of standard English grammar and usage when writing or speaking.
2. Demonstrate command of the conventions of standard English capitalization, punctuation, and spelling when writing.

Knowledge of Language

3. Use knowledge of language and its conventions when writing, speaking, reading, or listening.

Vocabulary Acquisition and Use

4. Determine or clarify the meaning of unknown and multiple-meaning words and phrases based on *grade 2 reading and content*, choosing flexibly from an array of strategies.
   a. Use sentence-level context as a clue to the meaning of a word or phrase.
   b. Determine the meaning of the new word formed when a known prefix is added to a known word.
   c. Use a known root word as a clue to the meaning of an unknown words with the same root.
   d. Use knowledge of the meaning of individual words to predict the meaning of compound words.
5. Demonstrate understanding of word relationships and nuances in word meanings.
   a. Identify real-life connections between words and their use.
   b. Distinguish shades of meaning among closely related verbs.
6. Use words and phrases acquired through conversations, reading and being read to, and responding to texts, including using adjectives and adverbs to describe.

Synonyms ■ Part 1

A **synonym** is a word that means the same or almost the same as another word.

Read each sentence.
Trace the word.
Then read the sentences again.

Word Bank	
argue	choose
exit	glide
keep	rush
shut	slice
trace	wish

1. To **argue** means to fight using words. _argue_

2. When you **choose** something, you pick the one you want. _choose_

3. To **exit** a place means to leave it. _exit_

4. To **glide** means to move smoothly and easily. _glide_

5. When you **keep** something, you save it. _keep_

6. You **rush** when you are in a hurry. _rush_

7. When you **shut** a door, you close it. _shut_

8. When you **slice** bread, you cut it into thin pieces. _slice_

9. To **trace** something, you follow the lines to copy it. _trace_

10. When you **wish** for something, you hope it will happen. _wish_

240 Vocabulary Words Kids Need to Know: 2nd Grade © 2012 by Scholastic Inc.

NAME _____   DATE _____

Synonyms ▪ Part 2

A. Write the best word to complete each sentence.

1. I saw the bird ___glide___ in the sky.

2. I ___wish___ I could go to the moon.

3. My mother likes to ___keep___ the pictures I draw.

4. We always ___shut___ the window when it rains.

5. When my sisters can't agree, sometimes they ___argue___.

6. When the movie was over, we had to ___exit___ the theater.

B. Cross out the word in each row that does not belong.

1.	cut	slice	~~slip~~
2.	~~creep~~	rush	speed
3.	~~choose~~	pick	~~wind~~
4.	~~face~~	draw	trace

OK

Synonyms ■ Part 3

Think of a synonym for each boldfaced word in the sentence. Use the Word Bank.

Complete the puzzle.

Word Bank

argue	choose
exit	glide
keep	rush
shut	slice
trace	wish

Across

4. I **skate** on the ice.

5. After class, we **leave** the room.

7. It's my turn to **pick** the game.

9. I am late so I must **hurry**.

10. My grandma will **cut** the pie.

Down

1. I **fight** with my brother when we don't agree.

2. We **want** to see the new movie soon.

3. Be sure to **save** your best work.

6. I am trying to **copy** the picture.

8. Remember to **close** the door when you leave.

240 Vocabulary Words Kids Need to Know: 2nd Grade © 2012 by Scholastic Inc.

Synonyms ■ Part 1

> A **synonym** is a word that means the same
> or almost the same as another word.

Read each sentence.
Trace the word.
Then read the sentences again.

Word Bank

breezy	bright
cozy	damp
grumpy	hefty
icy	puzzled
sleepy	simple

1. The wind blows on a **breezy** day. breezy

2. A **bright** day is one that has a lot of light. bright

3. When you are **cozy**, you feel snug and warm. cozy

4. When something is **damp**, it is a bit wet. damp

5. When you feel **grumpy**, you are
   unhappy and in a bad mood. grumpy

6. Something **hefty** is large or strong. hefty

7. An **icy** day is one that is very, very cold. icy

8. When you feel **puzzled**, you are
   confused, or do not understand something. puzzled

9. When you feel **sleepy**, you are tired. sleepy

10. When something is **simple**, it is easy. simple

NAME _____ DATE _____

Synonyms ■ Part 2

A. Write the best word to complete each sentence.

breezy	bright
cozy	damp
grumpy	hefty
icy	puzzled
sleepy	simple

1. I went to bed when I felt _____cozy_____ .

2. The _____grumpy_____ child was frowning.

3. We flew our kite on a _____breezy_____ day.

4. When it is _____bright_____ outside, I wear sunglasses.

5. It is _____simple_____ to make a peanut butter and jelly sandwich.

6. I was _____puzzled_____ and didn't know the answer.

B. Read each question. Choose the best answer. ✔

1. What do you wear on an **icy** day? ☐ swimsuit ☑ coat

2. Which one is **hefty**? ☑ elephant ☐ hamster

3. Which one feels **damp**? ☐ paper ☑ sponge

4. Which one is **cozy**? ☑ bed ☐ playground

240 Vocabulary Words Kids Need to Know: 2nd Grade © 2012 by Scholastic Inc.

NAME _____   DATE _____

Synonyms ■ Part 3

Read the clues.
Write the word next to its clue.
Find and circle the word in the puzzle.

Word Bank

| breezy | bright | cozy | damp | grumpy |
| hefty | icy | puzzled | sleepy | simple |

1. big and heavy _hefty_

2. snug and warm _cozy_

3. tired _sleepy_

4. confused _puzzled_

5. a little wet _damp_

6. with a lot of sunlight _bright_

7. not feeling happy _grumpy_

8. easy _simple_

9. some wind blowing _breezy_

10. freezing cold _icy_

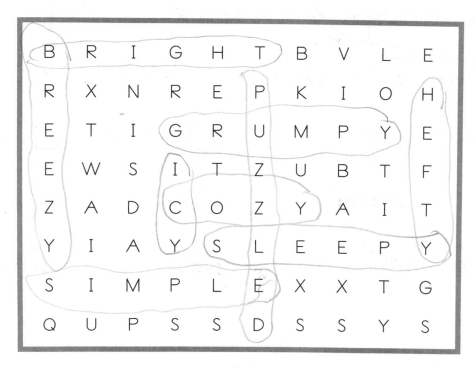

B R I G H T B V L E
R X N R E P K I O H
E T I G R U M P Y E
E W S I T Z U B T F
Z A D C O Z Y A I T
Y I A Y S L E E P Y
S I M P L E X X T G
Q U P S S D S S Y S

Antonyms ■ Part 1

| An **antonym** is a word that means the opposite of another word.

Read each sentence.
Trace the word.
Then read the sentences again.

1. When you **fix** something, you put it back together. fix

2. When you **wreck** something, you break it. wreck

3. When you feel sad, you **frown**. frown

4. When you feel happy, you **smile**. smile

5. When you **hide** something, people cannot see it. hide

6. When you **show** something, people can see it. show

7. When you **whisper**, you speak quietly. whisper

8. When you **yell**, you speak loudly. yell

9. When you think something is very sad, you **weep**. weep

10. When you think something is funny, you **laugh**.  laugh

12

NAME _____ DATE _____

Antonyms ■ Part 2

240 Vocabulary Words Kids Need to Know: 2nd Grade © 2012 by Scholastic Inc.

Word Bank

fix ⟷ wreck
frown ⟷ smile
hide ⟷ show
whisper ↔ yell
weep ⟷ laugh

A. Write the best word to complete each sentence.

1. When my mom hugs me I ___smile___ .

2. We ___yell___ when our team makes a good play.

3. I ___weep___ when I forget to bring my lunch.

4. When the teacher tells a joke, the children ___laugh___ .

5. I ___whisper___ when I don't want to wake up my brother.

6. Our parents ___hide___ the presents so we can't find them.

7. The deer ___wreck___ the garden when they eat the flowers.

B. Write the word that is the antonym of each picture.

1.  ___weep___

2.  ___fix___

3.  ___show___

13

Antonyms ■ Part 3

Cut out the squares on the right side of the page.

Match the word on each square to its antonym.

Glue the squares on the left side of the page to find the hidden picture.

frown	smile
hide	show
weep	laugh
yell	**whisper**
fix	wreck

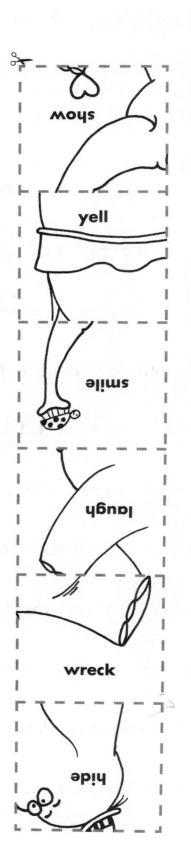

show

yell

smile

laugh

wreck

hide

240 Vocabulary Words Kids Need to Know: 2nd Grade © 2012 by Scholastic Inc.

Antonyms ■ Part 1

Word Bank

bland ⟷ spicy
dark ⟷ light
early ⟷ late
huge ⟷ tiny
loud ⟷ quiet

▌ An **antonym** is a word that means the opposite of another word.

Read each sentence.
Trace the word.
Then read the sentences again.

1. Food that tastes plain is **bland**. bland

2. **Spicy** food has a lot of flavor. spicy

3. At night, it is **dark** outside. dark

4. In the day, it is **light** outside. light

5. When you are **early**, you arrive before something starts. early

6. When you are **late**, you arrive after something starts. late

7. Something very, very big is **huge**. huge

8. Something very, very small is **tiny**. tiny

9. When there is a lot of noise, it is **loud**. loud

10. When there is no noise, it is **quiet**. quiet

Antonyms ■ Part 2

Word Bank

bland ⟷ spicy
dark ⟷ light
early ⟷ late
huge ⟷ tiny
loud ⟷ quiet

A. Write the best word to complete each sentence.

1. It is very _**quiet**_ in the library.

2. Pink and yellow are _**light**_ colors.

3. The _**spicy**_ food burned my mouth.

4. I was the first student to get to school. I was _**early**_.

5. I felt sick so I had to eat _**bland**_ food.

6. We missed the beginning of the movie because we were _**late**_.

B. Read each question. Choose the best answer. ✔

1. Which one is **tiny**?   ☐ dinosaur   ☑ ant

2. Which one is **loud**?   ☑ horn   ☐ giggle

3. Which one is **huge**?   ☑ castle   ☐ dollhouse

4. What can you see when it's **dark** outside?   ☑ moon   ☐ sun

240 Vocabulary Words Kids Need to Know: 2nd Grade © 2012 by Scholastic Inc.

Antonyms ■ Part 3

Read the word on each puzzle piece.
Draw a line to match each word with an antonym.

1. light   spicy

2. tiny   quiet

3. bland   dark

4. early   late

5. loud   huge

240 Vocabulary Words Kids Need to Know: 2nd Grade © 2012 by Scholastic Inc.

Verbs ■ Part 1

A **verb** describes an action.

Read each sentence.
Trace the word.
Then read the sentences again.

Think about how the verbs are alike and how they are different.

Word Bank

creep	stroll
rest	nap
take	grab
turn	spin
stir	whisk

1. To **creep** is to walk very slowly. creep

2. To **stroll** is to walk at a medium pace. stroll

3. To **rest** is to stay quiet until you feel like doing something again. rest

4. To **nap** is to sleep for a short time. nap

5. To **take** means to get something using your hands. take

6. To **grab** means to take something quickly. grab

7. To **turn** means to move in a circle. turn

8. To **spin** means to turn quickly, many times. spin

9. To **stir** something means to mix it by moving it around with a spoon or a stick. stir

10. To **whisk** something means to stir it quickly in one direction. whisk

240 Vocabulary Words Kids Need to Know: 2nd Grade © 2012 by Scholastic Inc.

Verbs ■ Part 2

A. Write the best word to complete each sentence.

1. I always _____take_____ my lunch to school.

2. I need to _____rest_____ after I run a lot.

3. I saw a spider _____spin_____ up the wall.

4. Watch the baby, or he may _____grab_____ the dog's tail.

5. We like to _____spin_____ in circles and fall down on the grass.

6. The water will come out of the faucet when you _____turn_____ the handle.

B. Read each question. Choose the best answer. ✔

1. Which food would you **stir**?   ☐ crackers   ☑ soup

2. Which food would you **whisk**?   ☑ eggs   ☐ toast

3. Where would you **stroll**?   ☑ park   ☐ pool

4. Where would you **nap**?   ☐ kitchen   ☑ bedroom

Verbs ■ Part 3

Fill in the chart with two words that match each definition.

Use the Word Bank.

Word Bank

creep	grab
rest	whisk
take	spin
turn	stroll
stir	nap

	Word 1	Word 2
1. Words to describe what you might do when you dance.	spih	turn
2. Words to describe what you might do when you cook.	stih	whisk
3. Words to describe what you might do when you relax.	hap	rest
4. Words to describe how you might pick something up.	grab	take
5. Words to describe how you might walk.	creep	stroll

240 Vocabulary Words Kids Need to Know: 2nd Grade © 2012 by Scholastic Inc.

Verbs ■ Part 1

▌ A **verb** describes an action.

Read each sentence.
Trace the word.
Then read the sentences again.

Think about how the verbs are alike and how they are different.

1. When you **climb**, you go to a higher place.   climb

2. To **nibble** is to take very small bites.   nibble

3. To **peek** is to look at something quickly.   peek

4. To **pounce** is to jump on something quickly.   pounce

5. To **scurry** is to run with short, quick steps.   scurry

6. When you **stare**, you look at something for a long time.   stare

7. To **stretch** is to spread out a part of your body.   stretch

8. To **surprise** is to do something without warning.   surprise

9. When you **wiggle**, you make small movements from side to side or up and down.   wiggle

10. When you **worry**, you think something bad might happen.   worry

240 Vocabulary Words Kids Need to Know: 2nd Grade © 2012 by Scholastic Inc.

NAME _____ DATE _____

Verbs ■ Part 2

Word Bank

climb	nibble
peek	pounce
scurry	stare
stretch	surprise
wiggle	worry

A. Write the best word to complete each sentence.

1. The cat went to _~~climb~~ peek_ into the kitchen.

2. He saw the mouse _nibble_ a piece of cheese.

3. The cat wanted to _surprise_ the mouse and catch him.

4. The mouse saw the cat _climb_ up onto a chair.

5. Before the cat could _pounce_, the mouse was able to _scurry_ out of the kitchen.

6. The mouse was safe and didn't need to _worry_.

B. Cross out the word in each row that does not belong.

1.	(climb)	look	stare
2.	eat	nibble	(run)
3.	(jump)	twist	wiggle
4.	pull	(sniff)	stretch

240 Vocabulary Words Kids Need to Know: 2nd Grade © 2012 by Scholastic Inc.

Verbs ▪ Part 3

Read the clues.

Write the word next to its clue.

Find and circle the word
in the puzzle.

Word Bank

climb	nibble	peek	pounce	scurry
stare	stretch	surprise	wiggle	worry

1. look for a long time
   _____ stare _____

2. eat small bites ___ nibble ___

3. twist around ___ wiggle ___

4. shock or startle
   _____ surprise _____

5. run away ___ scurry ___

6. feel upset ___ worry ___

7. jump on ___ pounce ___

8. a quick look ___ peek ___

9. go up high ___ climb ___

10. spread out
    _____ stretch _____

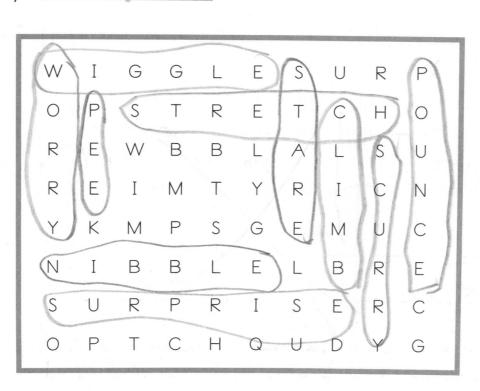

W	I	G	G	L	E	S	U	R	P
O	P	S	T	R	E	T	C	H	O
R	E	W	B	B	L	A	L	S	U
R	E	I	M	T	Y	R	I	C	N
Y	K	M	P	S	G	E	M	U	C
N	I	B	B	L	E	L	B	R	E
S	U	R	P	R	I	S	E	R	C
O	P	T	C	H	Q	U	D	Y	G

240 Vocabulary Words Kids Need to Know: 2nd Grade © 2012 by Scholastic Inc.

NAME _____ DATE _____

Verbs ■ Part 1

A **verb** describes an action.

Read each sentence.
Trace the word.
Then read the sentences again.

Think about how the verbs are alike and how they are different.

Word Bank

crawl	fade
fasten	flutter
gaze	scoot
soar	sprinkle
twist	yank

1. To **crawl** means to move on your hands and knees. crawl

2. To **fade** means to lose color. fade

3. To **fasten** means to attach one thing to something else. fasten

4. To **flutter** means to wave or flap something. flutter

5. To **gaze** at something means to look at it for a period of time. gaze

6. To **scoot** is a way to move quickly. scoot

7. To **soar** is to fly very high in the air. soar

8. To **sprinkle** is to scatter something in small drops or bits. sprinkle

9. To **twist** means to turn or bend something. twist

10. To **yank** means to pull something in a sharp way. yank

240 Vocabulary Words Kids Need to Know: 2nd Grade © 2012 by Scholastic Inc.

Verbs ■ Part 2

A. Write the best word to complete each sentence.

1. I tried to _____fasten_____ the buttons on my shirt.

2. I like to _____gaze_____ at the birds flying in the sky.

3. You must _____twist_____ off the cap to open the bottle.

4. The baby learned to _____crawl_____ before he learned to walk.

5. Mom told us to _____scoot_____, or we might be late for school.

6. My little sister tried to _____yank_____ the toy out of my hand.

B. Read each question. Choose the best answer. ✔

1. What would **flutter**? ☐ songs ☑ butterfly

2. Where would you **soar**? ☑ sky ☐ ground

3. What could you **sprinkle**? ☐ rake ☑ water

4. What could **fade**? ☐ shin ☑ shirt

NAME _____ DATE _____

Verbs ▪ Part 3

Read the clues.

Write the vocabulary word.

Use the answers in the boxes to complete
the puzzle below.

1. to look at for a long time g [a] z e

2. how babies move around [c] r a w l

3. to hook or button f a s [t] e n

4. to pour a little bit s p r [i] n k l e

5. to move quickly s c [o] o t

6. to pull sharply y a [n] k

7. to turn something around t [w] i s t

8. how birds move around in the sky s [o] a r

9. how a flag might move in the wind f l u t t e [r]

10. to lose color f a [d] e

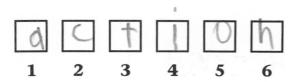

a c t i o n

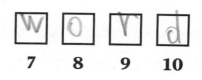

w o r d

1 2 3 4 5 6   7 8 9 10

NAME _____   DATE _____

Texture Words ■ Part 1

■ These words all describe a **texture**, or how something feels (or looks).

Read each sentence.
Trace the word.
Then read the sentences again.

Think about how the words are alike and how they are different.

Word Bank

chewy	crumbly
creamy	foamy
furry	gritty
rough	sharp
slimy	wrinkled

1. Something **chewy** can get stuck in your teeth. *chewy*

2. When something is **crumbly**, it falls apart easily. *crumbly*

3. When something is **creamy**, it is very soft and smooth. *creamy*

4. Something **foamy** has a lot of small bubbles in it. *foamy*

5. When something is **furry**, it has soft, thick hair. *furry*

6. When something is **gritty**, it feels like sand. *gritty*

7. When something is **rough**, there are bumps on its surface. *rough*

8. When something is **sharp**, it has a pointed end. *sharp*

9. Something **slimy** feels smooth, cold, and wet. *slimy*

10. When something is **wrinkled**, it has a lot of folds or lines. *wrinkled*

NAME _____ DATE _____

Texture Words ■ Part 2

Word Bank

chewy	crumbly
creamy	foamy
furry	gritty
rough	sharp
slimy	wrinkled

A. Write the best word to complete each sentence.

1. I like to pet the ___furry___ kitten.

2. Bubbles in the bathtub are ___foamy___.

3. Dad ironed the ___rough___ clothes.

4. When I touched the frog, it felt ___slimy___.

5. Peanut butter can be ___chewy___ or crunchy.

6. Mom told us to be careful with the ___sharp___ scissors.

B. Read each question. Choose the best answer. ✔

1. What feels **gritty**?   ✔ beach   ☐ swings

2. What feels **rough**?   ✔ bark   ☐ window

3. Which one is **crumbly**?   ✔ cookie   ☐ lollipop

4. Which one is **chewy**?   ☐ ice cream   ✔ gum

240 Vocabulary Words Kids Need to Know: 2nd Grade © 2012 by Scholastic Inc.

Texture Words ■ Part 3

Read the word on each puzzle piece.

Draw a line to match each word with something of that texture.

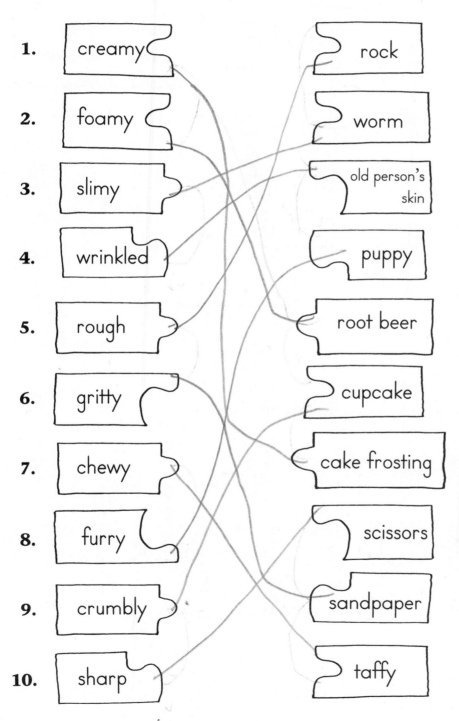

1. creamy

2. foamy

3. slimy

4. wrinkled

5. rough

6. gritty

7. chewy

8. furry

9. crumbly

10. sharp

rock

worm

old person's skin

puppy

root beer

cupcake

cake frosting

scissors

sandpaper

taffy

NAME _____ DATE _____

Sound Words ■ Part 1

These words all describe **sounds**.

Read each sentence.
Trace the word.
Then read the sentences again.

Think about how the sound words are alike and how they are different.

1. **Achoo** is the sound you make when you sneeze. <u>achoo</u>

2. A **chirp** is the sound you hear when a bird sings. <u>chirp</u>

3. A **click** is a sharp, quick sound. <u>click</u>

4. Dry leaves **crackle** when you walk on them. <u>crackle</u>

5. When a timer goes off, you hear a **ding**. <u>ding</u>

6. A **plink** is the sound rain makes when it hits the roof. <u>plink</u>

7. A **quack** is the sound a duck makes. <u>quack</u>

8. When a frog jumps into water, you hear a **splash**. <u>splash</u>

9. A **squeak** is a very short, high noise. <u>squeak</u>

10. When something goes by you very fast, you hear a **whoosh**. <u>whoosh</u>

240 Vocabulary Words Kids Need to Know: 2nd Grade © 2012 by Scholastic Inc.

Sound Words ■ Part 2

Word Bank

achoo	chirp
click	crackle
ding	plink
quack	splash
squeak	whoosh

A. Write the best word to complete each sentence.

1. I hear the ___crackle___ of the fire in the fireplace.

2. Every time I close the old door, I hear a ___click___.

3. I hear the water ___splash___ when I wash the dishes.

4. The sound of a ___quack___ tells me there is a duck nearby.

5. She heard a ___chirp___ and knew there was a bird outside her window.

6. When you hear the ___ding___, it's time to take the cake out of the oven.

B. Read each question. Choose the best answer. ✔

1. What do you need when you hear **plink, plink, plink**? ☐ sunscreen ☑ umbrella

2. What do you need when you hear **achoo**? ☑ tissue ☐ notebook paper

3. What could make a **click**? ☐ crayon ☑ computer mouse

4. What could make a **whoosh**? ☐ feather ☑ car

NAME _____ DATE _____

Sound Words ■ Part 3

Look at the pictures.
Write the best sound word in each speech balloon.

1.  *chirp*

2. *plink*

3. *splash*

4. *click*

5. *crackle*

6. *quack*

7. *achoo*

8. *whoosh*

9. *squeak*

10. *ding*

Homophones ■ Part 1

Word Bank

hole ⟷ whole
pair ⟷ pear
rap ⟷ wrap
sail ⟷ sale
steal ⟷ steel

A **homophone** is a word that sounds like another word but has a different meaning and a different spelling.

Read each sentence.
Trace the word.
Then read the sentences again.

1. A **hole** is a place where there is an empty space. hole

2. **Whole** means all of something, with nothing missing. whole

3. When two things match, they are a **pair**. pair

4. A **pear** is a sweet fruit that is bigger around the bottom than at the top. pear

5. To **rap** on something means to knock on it. rap

6. When you **wrap** a gift, you cover it in pretty paper. wrap

7. To **sail** means to move on water using the power of the wind. sail

8. A **sale** is a time when a store sells things for less than they usually cost. sale

9. To **steal** means to take something that does not belong to you. steal

10. **Steel** is a hard, strong metal that is used to make buildings. steel

Homophones ■ Part 2

A. Write the best word to complete each sentence.

1. The boats ____sail____ in the lake.

2. The ball rolled into a deep ____hole____ and got stuck.

3 The store was having a big ____sale____.

4. Use paper, tape, and ribbon to ____wrap____ a present.

5. My two older brothers ate a ____whole____ pizza.

6. We ate a fruit salad, made with an apple, a banana, and a ____pear____.

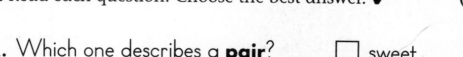

B. Read each question. Choose the best answer. ✔

1. Which one describes a **pair**? ☐ sweet ☑ two

2. What do you do when you **rap**? ☑ knock ☐ cover

3. What do people who **steal** do? ☑ take ☐ give

4. Which one is made of **steel**? ☐ cabin ☑ skyscraper

240 Vocabulary Words Kids Need to Know: 2nd Grade © 2012 by Scholastic Inc.

Homophones ■ Part 3

These notes are wrong.
Rewrite each note so it is correct.

1. Please water the pair tree.

   pear

2. The store will have a sail on gift rap in January.

   sale   wrap

3. Do not steel the hole pie! Save me a piece.

   whole

   steal

4. Do you want to sale with me at the lake?

   sail

5. Please wrap on the steal door.

   rap   steel

6. I will fix the whole in your pear of pants tonight.

   hole   pair

240 Vocabulary Words Kids Need to Know: 2nd Grade © 2012 by Scholastic Inc.

Homonyms ■ Part 1

┃ A **homonym** is a word that sounds like another
word, and can be spelled the same way, but has
a different meaning.

Read each sentence.
Trace the word.
Then read the sentences again.

Word Bank

ball ⟷ ball

bat ⟷ bat

pitcher ⟷ pitcher

row ⟷ row

sign ⟷ sign

1. A **ball** is a round object used to play different games. ball

2. A **ball** is a big party where people dance. ball

3. A **bat** is a long hard stick you use to hit a ball. bat

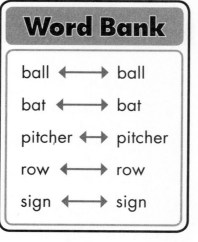

4. A flying animal that feeds at night is called a **bat**. bat

5. In baseball, the **pitcher** throws the ball to the batter. pitcher

6. A **pitcher** is a container that holds something you drink. pitcher

7. A **row** is a line of things or people side by side. row

8. To **row** a boat, you use oars to make it move through water. row

9. A **sign** is writing or a picture that gives you information. sign

10. When you write your name on something, you **sign** it. sign

240 Vocabulary Words Kids Need to Know: 2nd Grade © 2012 by Scholastic Inc.

Homonyms ■ Part 2

A. Write the best word to complete each sentence.

1. I put my stuffed animals in a ____row____ on the shelf.

2. The baseball player held a ____bat____ made of wood.

3. Cinderella dressed up and went to a ____ball____.

4. The ____pitcher____ threw the ____ball____ to the batter.

5. I remembered to ____sign____ my name at the bottom of the letter.

6. Let's ____row____ the boat to the other side of the lake.

B. Read each question. Choose the best answer. ✔

1. Can a bat hold a **bat**? ☐ yes ☑ no

2. Can a pitcher use a **pitcher**? ☑ yes ☐ no

3. Can you sign a **sign**? ☑ yes ☐ no

240 Vocabulary Words Kids Need to Know: 2nd Grade © 2012 by Scholastic Inc.

Homonyms ■ Part 3

Word Bank

ball ⟷ ball

bat ⟷ bat

pitcher ⟷ pitcher

row ⟷ row

sign ⟷ sign

Write the word that goes with each picture.

1. _____ sign _____

2. _____ ball _____

3.  _____ bat _____

4.  _____ row _____

5.  _____ sign _____

6. _____ pitcher _____

7.  _____ row _____

8. _____ pintcher _____

9. _____ bat _____

10. _____ ball _____

NAME _____ DATE _____

Compound Words ▪ Part 1

▌ A **compound word** is made up of two smaller words put together.

Read each sentence.
Trace the word.
Then read the sentences again.

1. A house for birds is called a **birdhouse**. *birdhouse*

2. A **cowboy** is someone who looks after cattle. *cowboy*

3. A **drumstick** is a stick used to play a drum. *drumstick*

4. A **firefly** is a small flying beetle that lights up at night. *firefly*

5. A farmer puts a **scarecrow** in a field to keep birds away. *scarecrow*

6. A **starfish** is a sea animal that looks like a star. *starfish*

7. A **sunflower** is a large flower with yellow petals and a dark center. *sunflower*

8. You use a **toothbrush** to clean your teeth. *toothbrush*

9. A **wheelchair** is a chair that moves on wheels. *wheelchair*

10. A **wristwatch** fits around your wrist and is used to tell time. *wristwatch*

Compound Words ■ Part 2

Word Bank

birdhouse	cowboy
drumstick	firefly
scarecrow	starfish
sunflower	toothbrush
wheelchair	wristwatch

A. Write the best word to complete each sentence.

1. My friend can't walk so he uses

   a ___wheelchair___.

2. Grandpa built a ___scarecrow___

   to put outside his window.

3. We saw a ___starfish___ when we visited the aquarium.

4. I look at my ___wristwatch___ when I want to know the time.

5. It's fun to watch the light of a ___toothbrush___ go

   on and off at night.

B. Write the two words that make up each compound word.

1. toothbrush   _____ + _____

2. drumstick   _____ + _____

3. sunflower   _____ + _____

4. cowboy   _____ + _____

5. scarecrow   _____ + _____

Compound Words ▪ Part 3

Draw a line to match each compound word
with its picture.

birdhouse	cowboy
drumstick	firefly
scarecrow	starfish
sunflower	toothbrush
wheelchair	wristwatch

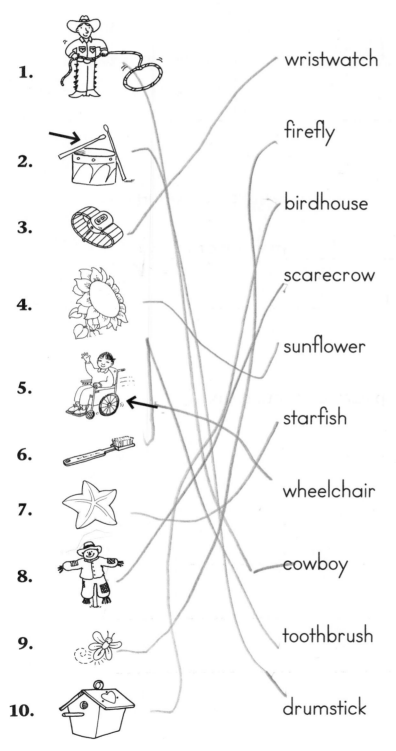

1.

2.

3.

4.

5.

6.

7.

8.

9.

10.

wristwatch

firefly

birdhouse

scarecrow

sunflower

starfish

wheelchair

cowboy

toothbrush

drumstick

Compound Words ■ Part 1

Word Bank

clothespin	goldfish
grasshopper	greenhouse
headphones	houseboat
playground	sidewalk
snowflake	wallpaper

| A **compound word** is made up of two smaller words put together.

Read each sentence.
Trace the word.
Then read the sentences again.

1. To clip clothes to a line to dry, you use a **clothespin**. clothespin

2. A small fish that is gold in color is a **goldfish**. goldfish

3. An insect that hops is a **grasshopper**. grasshopper

4. A **greenhouse** is a glass building in which plants can grow safely. greenhouse

5. You wear **headphones** over your ears to listen to music. headphones

6. A **houseboat** is a kind of boat that people can live in. houseboat

7. A **playground** is a place for children to play outside. playground

8. A **sidewalk** is a path for walking beside a street. sidewalk

9. A small bit of snow is called a **snowflake**. snowflake

10. **Wallpaper** is paper used to decorate a wall. wallpaper

240 Vocabulary Words Kids Need to Know: 2nd Grade © 2012 by Scholastic Inc.

NAME _____   DATE _____

Compound Words ■ Part 2

A. Write the best word to complete each sentence.

Word Bank	
clothespin	goldfish
grasshopper	greenhouse
headphones	houseboat
playground	sidewalk
snowflake	wallpaper

1. I roller skate on
   the _sidewalk_.

2. The _grasshopper_ was
   in the garden.

3. You can find a slide at a _playground_.

4. Today, I saw the first _snowflake_ of winter.

5. My uncle lives on a _greenhouse_ in the river.

6. I sometimes listen to music using _headphones_.

B. Use these words to make four compound words.

clothes   fish   green   gold   paper   house   pin   wall

1. _____

2. _____

3. _____

4. _____

Compound Words ■ Part 3

Think of a word for each picture.
Then write the compound word.

Word Bank

clothespin   goldfish
grasshopper   greenhouse
headphones   houseboat
playground   sidewalk
snowflake   wallpaper

1.  + flake = _snow_

2. gold + 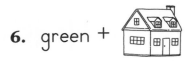 = _fish_

3. + phones = _head_

4. wall + = _paper_

5. + = _clothespin_

6. green + = _house_

7. + ground = _play_

8. side +  = _walk_

9. + hopper = _grass_

10. +  = _houseboat_

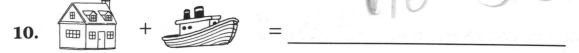

44

NAME _____   DATE _____

Prefixes *un-, re-* ■ Part 1

A **prefix** is a word part that is added to the beginning of a word. A prefix changes the meaning of a word.

The prefix *un-* means "not."

The prefix *re-* means "again."

Word Bank

uneven	unhappy
unpack	unsafe
untrue	remake
replace	reread
reuse	rewrite

Read each sentence.
Trace the word.
Then read the sentences again.

1. Something **uneven** is not level. ~~uneven~~

2. **Unhappy** means to be sad. ~~unhappy~~

3. **Unpack** means to empty something, like a suitcase after a trip. ~~unpack~~

4. Something **unsafe** is dangerous. ~~unsafe~~

5. Something false is **untrue**. ~~untrue~~

6. When you **remake** your bed, you make it again. ~~remake~~

7. When something is missing, you **replace** it. ~~replace~~

8. When you read a book again, you **reread** it. ~~reread~~

9. When you use something more than once, you **reuse** it. ~~reuse~~

10. When you erase a word and write it again, you **rewrite** it.

240 Vocabulary Words Kids Need to Know: 2nd Grade © 2012 by Scholastic Inc.

Prefixes *un-*, *re-* ■ Part 2

Word Bank

uneven	unhappy
unpack	unsafe
untrue	remake
replace	reread
reuse	rewrite

A. Write the best word to complete each sentence.

1. I save something so I can ___reuse___ it.

2. He likes to ___reread___ his favorite books.

3. If you tell a lie, what you say is ___untrue___.

4. My sandwich fell apart so I had to ___remake___ it.

5. When my little sister was crying, I knew she was ___unhappy___.

6. My mom told me that it is ___unsafe___ to swim in a pool alone.

B. Read each question. Choose the best answer. ✔

1. Which one can you **rewrite**?   ☐ pencil   ☑ story

2. When do you **unpack**?   ☑ after a trip   ☐ before a trip

3. Which one would you **replace**?   ☑ broken toy   ☐ new toy

4. Which one describes something **uneven**?   ☐ straight   ☑ crooked

240 Vocabulary Words Kids Need to Know: 2nd Grade © 2012 by Scholastic Inc.

Prefixes *un-*, *re-* ■ Part 3

Think of a word for each clue.
Use the Word Bank.
Complete the puzzle.

Word Bank

| uneven | unhappy | unpack | unsafe | untrue |
| remake | replace | reread | reuse | rewrite |

Across

3. sad; not happy

4. dangerous; not safe

7. to read again

8. to write again

Down

1. to make something again

2. to put a new thing in the place of an old thing

3. to take things out of a box, bag, or suitcase

4. not level or even

5. false; not true

6. to use again

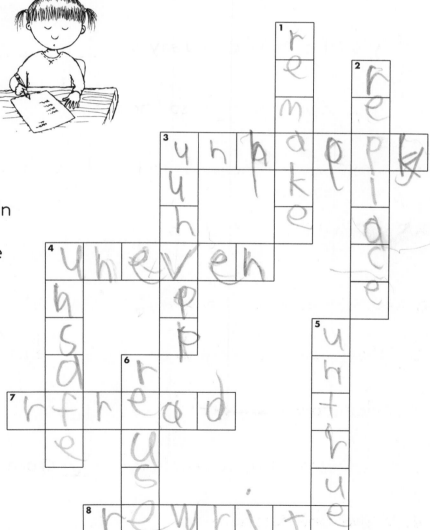

240 Vocabulary Words Kids Need to Know: 2nd Grade © 2012 by Scholastic Inc.

Suffixes *-ful, -er* ■ Part 1

Word Bank	
careful	colorful
hopeful	joyful
playful	baker
builder	painter
singer	writer

▌ A **suffix** is a word part that is added to the end of a word. A suffix changes the meaning of a word.

The suffix *-ful* means "full of."

The suffix *-er* means "a person who acts as."

Read each sentence.
Trace the word.
Then read the sentences again.

1. Being **careful** means paying close attention to what you do.   *careful*

2. Something **colorful** is made up of many colors.   *colorful*

3. Being **hopeful** means that you wish for something.   *hopeful*

4. When you are **joyful**, you feel very happy.   *joyful*

5. Being **playful** means you like to play and have fun.   *playful*

6. A **baker** is a person who bakes foods.   *baker*

7. A **builder** is a person whose job it is to build things.   *builder*

8. A **painter** is a person who paints.   *painter*

9. A **singer** is a person who sings songs.   *singer*

10. A **writer** is a person who writes things like stories.   *writer*

Suffixes *-ful, -er* ■ Part 2

A. Write the best word to complete each sentence.

Word Bank				
careful	colorful	hopeful	joyful	playful
baker	builder	painter	singer	writer

1. When I passed the test, I felt ____joyful____.

2. My friend drew a very ____colorful____ picture.

3. I was very ____careful____ when I crossed the street.

4. This dog is ____playful____. He likes to chase the ball.

5. My brother was ____hopeful____ that we might go to the amusement park.

B. Write the word that goes with each picture.

1. ____writer____

2. ____singer____

3. ____baker____

4. ____painter____

5. ____builder____

Suffixes -ful, -er ▪ Part 3

Read the clues.
Write the word next to its clue.
Find and circle the word in
the puzzle.

Word Bank				
careful	colorful	hopeful	joyful	playful
baker	builder	painter	singer	writer

1. someone who sings
   singer

2. feeling joy _joyful_

3. someone who paints
   painter

4. acting in a fun way
   playful

5. someone who makes a cake
   baker

6. feeling hope _hopeful_

7. acting with care
   careful

8. someone who writes a story
   writer

9. having a lot of color
   colorful

10. someone who builds a house
    builder

```
I X G B J M H C A R E F U L H
S L A P F U P O R E G U L R W
A P L A Y F U L K E B A K E R
I A O R F D J O Y F U L L T I
S I N G E R A R C L I U R E T
T N R H O P E F U L L D E R E
E T O R F X Y U F U D C X T R
R E T R I Q U L B D E C X T L
I R G B J M H C A M R F U L H
```

240 Vocabulary Words Kids Need to Know: 2nd Grade © 2012 by Scholastic Inc.

Character Traits ■ Part 1

Word Bank	
bossy	brave
curious	friendly
gentle	greedy
honest	mean
polite	sneaky

▌ **Character traits** tell what someone
is like or how he or she acts.

Read each sentence.
Trace the word.
Then read the sentences again.

1. A **bossy** person likes telling others what to do. bossy

2. A **brave** person acts strong and without fear. brave

3. A **curious** person likes to learn about things. curious

4. A **friendly** person acts nice and helpful. friendly

5. A **gentle** person is kind and careful with others. gentle

6. A **greedy** person does not like to share with others. greedy

7. An **honest** person tells the truth. honest

8. A **mean** person is not kind or friendly. mean

9. A **polite** person has good manners. polite

10. A **sneaky** person tries to do things in secret. sneaky

240 Vocabulary Words Kids Need to Know: 2nd Grade © 2012 by Scholastic Inc.

NAME _____ DATE _____

Character Traits ■ Part 2

Word Bank

bossy	brave
curious	friendly
gentle	greedy
honest	mean
polite	sneaky

A. Write the best word to complete each sentence.

1. He never lies. He is _____honest_____.

2. My friend was _____gentle_____ when he held his new puppy.

3. My _____bossy_____ sister always tries to tell me what to do.

4. She always says "please" and "thank you." She is _____polite_____.

5. I read a lot of books because I am _____curious_____ about many things.

6. The _____brave_____ firefighter saved the people who were caught in a fire.

B. Read each question. Choose the best answer. ✔

1. What does a **greedy** person like to do?   ☑ take   ☑ give

2. What does a **friendly** person's face show?   ☑ frown   ☑ smile

3. Which one is **mean**?   ☑ bully   ☑ friend

4. How might a **sneaky** person walk?   ☐ tiptoe   ☑ stomp

Character Traits ■ Part 3

Word Sort

Which words have good feelings connected to them?
Which words have bad feelings connected to them?
Sort the words in the Word Bank into two groups.
Write them in the chart.

Word Bank

bossy	brave
curious	friendly
gentle	greedy
honest	mean
polite	sneaky

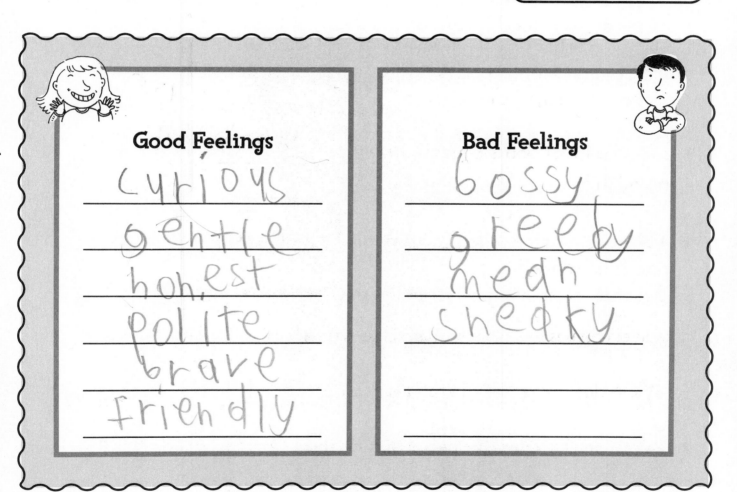

Good Feelings

curious
gentle
honest
polite
brave
friendly

Bad Feelings

bossy
greedy
mean
sneaky

240 Vocabulary Words Kids Need to Know: 2nd Grade © 2012 by Scholastic Inc.

Mealtime ■ Part 1

Word Bank	
meal	breakfast
lunch	dinner
drink	dessert
snack	leftovers
kitchen	cafeteria

Special words are used to tell
about **mealtime**.

Read each sentence.
Trace the word.
Then read the sentences again.

1. A **meal** is the food we eat at one time.   *meal*

2. **Breakfast** is a meal eaten in the morning.   *breakfast*

3. **Lunch** is a meal eaten in the middle of the day.   *lunch*

4. **Dinner** is a meal eaten in the evening.   *dinner*

5. You have a **drink** when you are thirsty.   *drink*

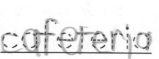

6. **Dessert** is something sweet eaten at the end of a meal.   *dessert*

7. A **snack** is something you eat between meals.   *snack*

8. The food not eaten at a meal is called **leftovers**.
   You can eat that food at another time.   *leftovers*

9. A **kitchen** is the room where you make a meal.   *kitchen*

10. At school, the **cafeteria** is a place where
    you can eat a meal.   *cafeteria*

240 Vocabulary Words Kids Need to Know: 2nd Grade © 2012 by Scholastic Inc.

Mealtime ■ Part 2

Word Bank	
meal	breakfast
lunch	dinner
drink	dessert
snack	leftovers
kitchen	cafeteria

A. Write the best word to complete each sentence.

1. For _____*lunch*_____ , she eats eggs and toast.

2. After _____*dinner*_____, I finish my homework.

3. Sometimes I buy my lunch in the _____*cafeteria*_____.

4. For _____*dessert*_____ , he eats a sandwich and a banana.

5. At my house, we only eat _____*dessert*_____ on special days.

6. Tomorrow, we will eat the _____*leftovers*_____ from tonight's meal.

B. Read each question. Choose the best answer. ✔

1. Which one is in a **kitchen**? ☑ car   ☐ oven

2. Which one is a **drink**? ☑ lemon   ☐ lemonade

3. Which one is a **snack**? ☐ apple   ☑ cheeseburger

4. What do you do during a **meal**? ☐ cook food   ☑ eat food

Mealtime ■ Part 3

Think of the best word to complete each sentence.
Use the Word Bank. Complete the puzzle.

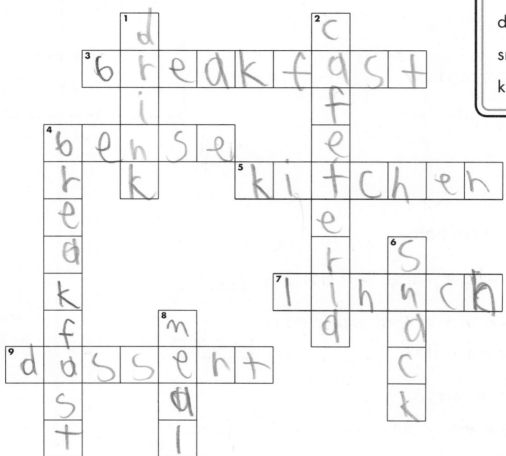

Across

3. I always eat cereal for ___.

4. Most days, I take my ___ to school.

5. We make food in the ___.

7. Sometimes, I can invite a
   friend to ___.

9. Ice cream makes a good ___.

Down

1. Orange juice is my favorite ___.

2. At school, I eat in the ___.

4. We have some ___ in
   the refrigerator.

6. I eat a ___ before soccer practice.

8. On Thanksgiving, we have
   a special ___.

On Vacation ■ Part 1

Word Bank	
camp	hotel
map	passport
sleepover	suitcase
ticket	travel
vacation	visit

Special words are used to tell about a **vacation**.

Read each sentence.
Trace the word.
Then read the sentences again.

1. A **camp** is a place with tents or cabins where you spend time outdoors.   camp

2. A **hotel** is a place where you can spend the night away from home.   hotel

3. A **map** shows where places or things are.   map

4. A **passport** is a booklet that proves you are a citizen of a country.   passport

5. A **sleepover** is when you spend the night at someone else's house.   sleepover

6. A **suitcase** is a bag to carry clothes in when you travel.   suitcase

7. A **ticket** is a piece of paper that shows you have paid to do something.   ticket

8. To **travel** is to go from one place to another place.   travel

9. **Vacation** is time away from school or work.   vacation

10. To **visit** is to go somewhere or see someone.   visit

NAME _____ DATE _____

On Vacation ■ Part 2

A. Write the best word to complete each sentence.

1. I like to _____visit_____ my grandparents.

2. We stayed at a _____hotel_____ when we went to the city.

3. I like to _____map_____ to different places.

4. During the summer, my family goes on a _____vacation_____.

5. When we go to a _____camp_____, we sleep in our sleeping bags.

6. On the weekend, I sometimes have a _____sleepover_____ at my friend's house.

B. Write the word that goes with each picture.

1.  passport

2.  ticket

3.  map

4. suitcase

240 Vocabulary Words Kids Need to Know: 2nd Grade © 2012 by Scholastic Inc.

On Vacation ■ Part 3

Think of the best word to complete each sentence.
Use the Word Bank. Complete the puzzle.

Across

2. During the ___ , we stayed up late.

4. Sometimes we ___ by train.

5. At ___ , we stay in a cabin.

7. I like to ___ the amusement park.

8. We need a ___ to find our way.

9. Summer ___ is my favorite time of year.

Down

1. We are staying at a ___ near the beach.

3. I unpack my ___ after a trip.

4. I give my ___ to the conductor.

6. I need a ___ to go to another country.

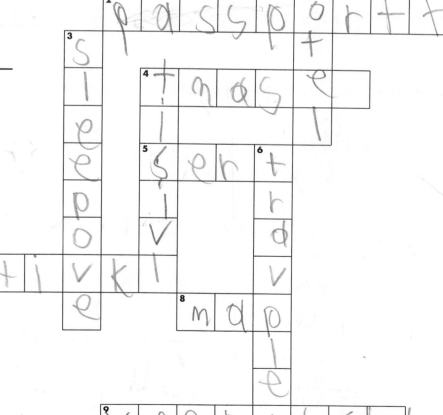

Land and Water ■ Part 1

Special words are used for different kinds of **land** formations and bodies of **water**.

Read each sentence.
Trace the word.
Then read the sentences again.

Word Bank

cave	dune
hill	lake
ocean	pond
mountain	range
river	stream

1. A **cave** is an open space in the side of a mountain or under the ground. <u>cave</u>

2. A **dune** is a mound of sand made by blowing winds. <u>dune</u>

3. A **hill** is a place where the land rises above the area around it. <u>hill</u>

4. A **lake** is water with land all around it. <u>lake</u>

5. An **ocean** is a very large body of saltwater. <u>ocean</u>

6. A **pond** is water with land all around it. It is smaller than a lake. <u>pond</u>

7. A **mountain** is a very high hill. <u>mountain</u>

8. A **range** is a group of mountains. <u>range</u>

9. A **river** is a large amount of flowing water. <u>river</u>

10. A **stream** is a small river. <u>stream</u>

240 Vocabulary Words Kids Need to Know: 2nd Grade © 2012 by Scholastic Inc.

Land and Water ■ Part 2

A. Write the best word to complete each sentence.

1. We saw a sand _____ hill _____ at the beach.

2. Bats live inside a _____ cave _____ .

3. Mount Everest is the world's tallest _____ moubtoin .

4. A _____ range _____ is made up of many mountains.

5. If there is snow, we like to sled down the _____ stree in the park.

6. When the small _____ pond _____ in the backyard freezes, we go ice skating.

B. Read each question. Choose the best answer. ✔

1. Which one is smaller?   ☐ ocean   ☑ river

2. Which one is smaller?   ☐ stream   ☑ river

3. Which one is larger?   ☑ lake   ☐ ocean

4. Which one is larger?   ☑ lake   ☐ pond

holow

Land and Water ■ Part 3

Some of the words name land formations.
Others name bodies of water.

Sort the words in the Word Bank into two groups.

Write them in the chart.

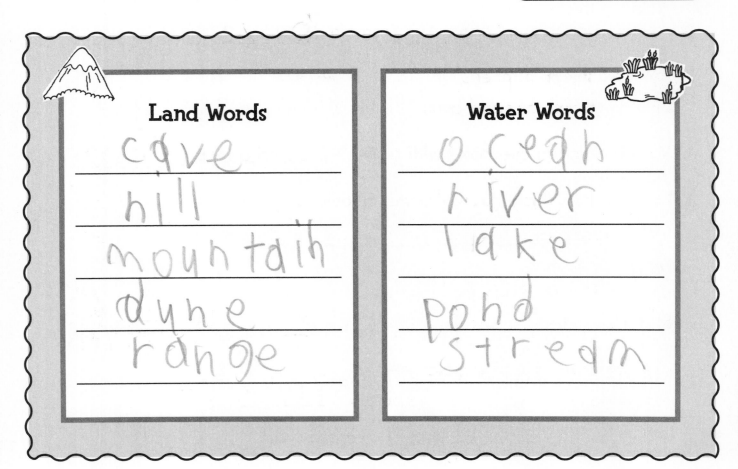

Land Words

cave
hill
mountain
dune
range

Water Words

ocean
river
lake
pond
stream

Super Weather ■ Part 1

Special words are used to describe different kinds of **weather**.

Read each sentence.
Trace the words.
Then read the sentences again.

Word Bank

blizzard	dust storm
flood	fog
hail	heat wave
hurricane	sleet
tidal wave	tornado

1. A **blizzard** is a very heavy snowstorm. *blizzard*

2. A **dust storm** happens when strong winds
   blow dust, soil, or sand around a large area. *dust storm*

3. When an area overflows with water it is called a **flood**. *flood*

4. **Fog** is a low, thick cloud of water droplets. *fog*

5. **Hail** is made of small balls of ice that fall from the sky. *hail*

6. A **heat wave** is very hot weather
   that lasts a few days. *heat wave*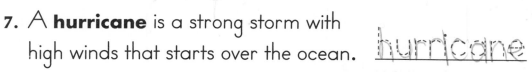

7. A **hurricane** is a strong storm with
   high winds that starts over the ocean. *hurricane*

8. **Sleet** is rain that is partly frozen. *sleet*

9. A **tidal wave** is a very large ocean wave
   that can cause a lot of flooding. *tidal wave*

10. A **tornado** is a powerful storm with strong winds
    that spin in the shape of a cone. *tornado*

240 Vocabulary Words Kids Need to Know: 2nd Grade © 2012 by Scholastic Inc.

NAME _____ DATE _____

Super Weather ■ Part 2

Word Bank

blizzard	dust storm
flood	fog
hail	heat wave
hurricane	sleet
tidal wave	tornado

A. Write the best words to complete each sentence.

1. After the ___blizzard___, we built a snowman.

2. It hurt when the ___hail___ hit my head.

3. During the ___flood___, the town was covered in water.

4. People had trouble breathing during the ___fog___.

5. We went swimming during the ___heat wave___ to cool off.

B. Cross out the word in each row that does not belong.

1.	~~tornado~~	twilight	twister
2.	ice	sleet	sunshine
3.	clear	cloud	fog
4.	rain	ocean	tidal wave
5.	hurricane	winter	wind

Super Weather ■ Part 3

Trace a path through the maze.
Follow the weather words.

240 Vocabulary Words Kids Need to Know: 2nd Grade © 2012 by Scholastic Inc.

Word Bank

blizzard	dust storm
flood	fog
hail	heat wave
hurricane	sleet
tidal wave	tornado

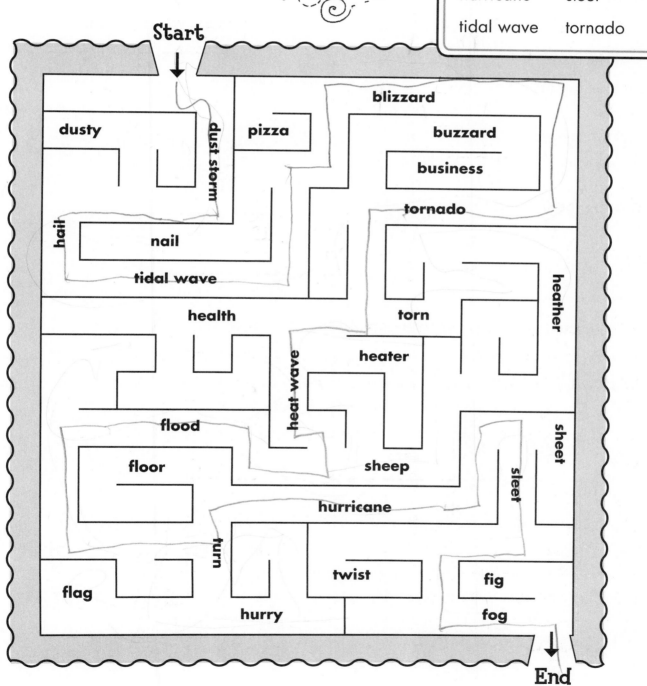

Start

dusty

dust storm

pizza

blizzard

buzzard

business

tornado

hail

nail

tidal wave

heather

health

torn

heat wave

heater

sheet

flood

sleet

floor

sheep

hurricane

turn

flag

twist

fig

hurry

fog

End

Land Animals ■ Part 1

Special words are used to name different kinds of **land animals**.

Read each sentence.
Trace the word.
Then read the sentences again.

Word Bank

camel	elephant
giraffe	gorilla
leopard	panda
polar bear	rhinoceros
tiger	zebra

1. A **camel** is a large animal with humps on its back. camel

2. An **elephant** is a very large, gray animal with big ears and a long nose called a trunk. elephant

3. A **giraffe** is a very tall animal with long, thin legs and a long neck. giraffe

4. A **gorilla** is a large ape with long arms. gorilla

5. A **leopard** is a large spotted animal in the cat family. leopard

6. A **panda** is not a bear, but it looks like one. It is known for its black and white fur. panda

7. A **polar bear** has white fur and lives in icy areas in the Arctic. polar bear

8. A **rhinoceros** is a large animal with a horn on its nose. rhinoceros

9. A **tiger** is a large striped animal from the cat family. tiger

10. A **zebra** is a large animal that looks like a horse. It has a mane and black and white stripes. zebra

240 Vocabulary Words Kids Need to Know: 2nd Grade © 2012 by Scholastic Inc.

Land Animals ■ Part 2

A. Write the best word to complete each sentence.

Word Bank

camel	elephant
giraffe	gorilla
leopard	panda
polar bear	rhinoceros
tiger	zebra

1. The _polar bea_'s fur keeps it warm on the ice.

2. An _elephant_ can hold water in its trunk.

3. A _camel_ can hold water in its humps.

4. The _zebra_ has stripes and a mane.

5. A _tiger_ is a large, wild cat with stripes.

6. The _panda_ is black and white and eats bamboo.

B. Read each question. Choose the best answer. ✔

1. Which one is in the cat family?   ☐ leopard   ☑ camel

2. Which one has long arms?   ☐ gorilla   ☑ giraffe

3. Which one has a horn?   ☑ elephant   ☐ rhinoceros

4. Which one is taller?   ☐ giraffe   ☑ tiger

NAME _____ DATE _____

Land Animals ■ Part 3

Read the riddle clues.
Write the word for each clue. Use the Word Bank.

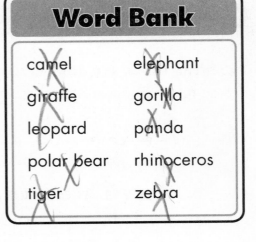

Word Bank

camel	elephant
giraffe	gorilla
leopard	panda
polar bear	rhinoceros
tiger	zebra

1. I am gray and have a trunk.
   What am I? _elephant_

2. I have stripes, fur, and a tail.
   What am I? _tiger_

3. I am white and can swim in icy
   water. What am I? _polahbear_

4. I am black and white and look like
   a bear. What am I? _panda_

5. I have a hump and live in the desert. What am I? _camel_

6. I am a large ape with long arms. What am I? _gorilla_

7. I am black and white and look like a horse.
   What am I? _zebra_

8. I am large and have a horn. What am I? _rhihoceros_

9. I have spots and a tail. What am I? _leopard_

10. I am very tall and have a long neck. What am I? _giraffe_

240 Vocabulary Words Kids Need to Know: 2nd Grade © 2012 by Scholastic Inc.

Garden ■ Part 1

Word Bank

bloom	bush
grass	hose
leaves	mower
rake	shovel
soil	worm

Special words are used to name things you might find in a **garden**.

Read each sentence.
Trace the word.
Then read the sentences again.

1. When flowers **bloom**, they open up. bloom

2. A **bush** is a plant with branches. It is smaller than a tree. bush

3. **Grass** is a green plant that spreads across the ground. grass

4. A **hose** is a long rubber tube that water goes through. hose

5. **Leaves** grow on plants and trees. They are usually green. leaves

6. You use a **mower** to cut grass. mower

7. A **rake** is a tool with a long handle and
   metal teeth used to gather fallen leaves. rake

8. A **shovel** is a tool with a handle and a scoop on the end. shovel

9. **Soil** is the top layer of earth that plants grow in. soil

10. A **worm** is a long, thin, soft animal that lives in the ground. worm

Garden Part 2

Word Bank

bloom	bush
grass	hose
leaves	mower
rake	shovel
soil	worm

A. Write the best word to complete each sentence.

1. The ___*sworm*___ wiggled through the soil.

2. Some ___*geaves*___ change color during Autumn.

3. We used a ___*hose*___ to water the plants.

4. The gardener uses a ___*shavel*___ to dig a hole in the ground.

5. The ___*bush*___ was long so I used a ___*rake*___ to cut it.

6. We saw two birds in the ___*grass*___ .

B. Cross out the word in each row that does not belong.

1.	leaves	~~mower~~	tree
2.	~~bloom~~	flower	grass
3.	dirt	soil	~~sun~~
4.	~~bark~~	rake	tool

240 Vocabulary Words Kids Need to Know: 2nd Grade © 2012 by Scholastic Inc.

Garden ■ Part 3

Write the word that goes with each picture.
Use the Word Bank.

1. _leaves_

2.  _worm_

3.  _shovel_

4. _mower_

5.  _bloom_

6. _grass_

7.  _hose_

8.  _soil_

9. _rak_

10. _bush_

Money ■ Part 1

Special words are used to tell about **money**.

Read each sentence.
Trace the words.
Then read the sentences again.

1. **Cash** is money. It includes coins and dollar bills. *cash*

2. A **coin** is a piece of metal that is used as money. *coin*

3. A **penny** is a small metal coin that equals 1 cent. *penny*

4. A **nickel** is a small metal coin that equals 5 cents. *nickel*

5. A **dime** is a very small metal coin that equals 10 cents. *dime*

6. A **quarter** is a metal coin that equals 25 cents. *quarter*

7. A **half-dollar** is a large metal coin that equals 50 cents. *half-dollar*

8. A **dollar bill** is paper money. It equals 100 cents. *dollar bill*

9. The **price** is how much money something costs. *price*

10. **Change** is money you get back when you pay for something. *change*

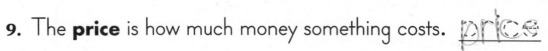

Money ■ Part 2

240 Vocabulary Words Kids Need to Know: 2nd Grade © 2012 by Scholastic Inc.

A. Write the word that goes with each picture.

Word Bank

cash	coin
penny	nickel
dime	quarter
half-dollar	dollar bill
price	change

1. penny

2. hicked

3. dime

4. quarter

5. half-dollar

6.  dolloh bill

B. Read each question. Choose the best answer. ✔

1. Which one tells how much something costs? ☑ change ☐ price

2. Which one could you find in a pocket? ☐ cash ☑ price

3. Which one tells about money you get back? ☑ price ☐ change

4. Which one makes more noise when it hits the floor? ☐ coin ☑ dollar bill

73

Money ■ Part 3

Read the clues.
Write the word next to its clue.
Find and circle the word in the puzzle.

1. metal money _coin_

2. paper money _dollar_

3. a coin worth 5 cents _penny_

4. a coin worth 50 cents _half dollar_

5. money left over after paying _change_

6. a coin worth 1 cent _nickel_

7. coins and bills _cash_

8. a coin worth 10 cents _dime_

9. a coin worth 25 cents _quarter_

10. the cost of something _price_

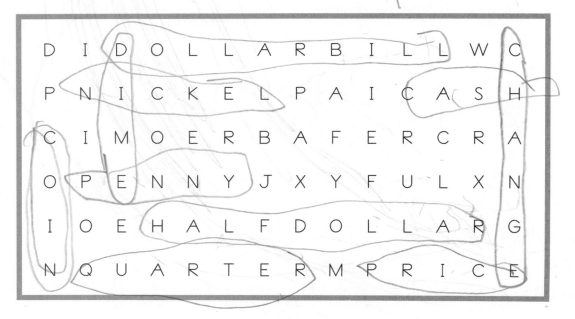

D I D O L L A R B I L L W C
P N I C K E L P A I C A S H
C I M O E R B A F E R C R A
O P E N N Y J X Y F U L X N
I O E H A L F D O L L A R G
N Q U A R T E R M P R I C E

Linear Measurement ■ Part 1

Word Bank	
measure	inch
foot	yard
mile	centimeter
meter	ruler
yardstick	meter stick

■ Special words are used for different units and tools of linear **measurement**.

Read each sentence.
Trace the word.
Then read the sentences again.

1. When you **measure** something, you find out about its size. ~~measure~~

2. An **inch** is a small unit of length |— ONE INCH —| ~~inch~~

3. A **foot** is equal to 12 inches. ~~foot~~   *3600*

4. A **yard** is equal to three feet. ~~yard~~

5. A **mile** is equal to 5,280 feet. It is used to measure distance. ~~mile~~

6. A **centimeter** is a small metric unit. |— ONE CENTIMETER —| ~~centimeter~~

7. A **meter** is a metric unit about as long as a baseball bat. ~~meter~~

8. To measure 12 inches, you use a **ruler**. ~~ruler~~

9. To measure 3 feet, you use a **yardstick**. ~~yardstick~~

10. To measure a centimeter or a meter, you use a **meter stick**. A meter stick is a little longer than a yardstick. ~~meter stick~~

NAME _____ DATE _____

Linear Measurement ■ Part 2

A. Write the best word to complete each sentence.

1. Three feet equals one __yard__ .

2. I __measure__ myself to find out how tall I am.

3. To find out the length of my shoe, I used a __meterstick__ .

4. We rode our bikes one __mile__ to the park.

B. Read each question. Choose the best answer. ✔

1. Which one is about the same length as a yard?   ☑ meter   ☐ mile

2. Which one equals 12 inches?   ☐ foot   ☑ meter

3. Which one is longer?   ☑ centimeter   ☐ inch

4. Which one is shorter?   ☐ centimeter   ☑ meter

5. A __meterstick__ is a measuring tool about as long as a __meter__

240 Vocabulary Words Kids Need to Know: 2nd Grade © 2012 by Scholastic Inc.

Linear Measurement ■ Part 3

Sort nine words in the Word Bank
into two groups.

Write them in the chart.

Word Bank

centimeter	yardstick
ruler	meter
mile	inch
meter stick	yard
foot	measure

Units of Measure	Tools Used to Measure
centimeter	ruler
mile	meter stick
foot	yardstick
meter	measure
inch	
yard	

WORD LIST

achoo, p. 30
argue, p. 6

baker, p. 48
ball, p. 36
ball, p. 36
bat, p. 36
bat, p. 36
birdhouse, p. 39
bland, p. 15
blizzard, p. 63
bloom, p. 69
bossy, p. 51
brave, p. 51
breakfast, p. 54
breezy, p. 9
bright, p. 9
builder, p. 48
bush, p. 69

cafeteria, p. 54
camel, p. 66
camp, p. 57
careful, p. 48
cash, p. 72
cave, p. 60
centimeter, p. 75
change, p. 72
chewy, p. 27
chirp, p. 30
choose, p. 6
click, p. 30
climb, p. 21
clothespin, p. 42
coin, p. 72
colorful, p. 48
cowboy, p. 39
cozy, p. 9
crackle, p. 30
crawl, p. 24
creamy, p. 27
creep, p. 18
crumbly, p. 27
curious, p. 51

damp, p. 9
dark, p. 15
dessert, p. 54
dime, p. 72
ding, p. 30
dinner, p. 54
dollar bill, p. 72

drink, p. 54
drumstick, p. 39
dune, p. 60
dust storm, p. 63

early, p. 15
elephant, p. 66
exit, p. 6

fade, p. 24
fasten, p. 24
firefly, p. 39
fix, p. 12
flood, p. 63
flutter, p. 24
foamy, p. 27
fog, p. 63
foot, p. 75
friendly, p. 51
frown, p. 12
furry, p. 27

gaze, p. 24
gentle, p. 51
giraffe, p. 66
glide, p. 6
goldfish, p. 42
gorilla, p. 66
grab, p. 18
grass, p. 69
grasshopper, p. 42
greedy, p. 51
greenhouse, p. 42
gritty, p. 27
grumpy, p. 9

hail, p. 63
half-dollar, p. 72
headphones, p. 42
heat wave, p. 63
hefty, p. 9
hide, p. 12
hill, p. 60
hole, p. 33
honest, p. 51
hopeful, p. 48
hose, p. 69
hotel, p. 57
houseboat, p. 42
huge, p. 15
hurricane, p. 63
icy, p. 9
inch, p. 75

joyful, p. 48

keep, p. 6
kitchen, p. 54

lake, p. 60
late, p. 15
laugh, p. 12
leaves, p. 69
leftovers, p. 54
leopard, p. 66
light, p. 15
loud, p. 15
lunch, p. 54

map, p. 57
meal, p. 54
mean, p. 51
measure, p. 75
meter, p. 75
meter stick, p. 75
mile, p. 75
mountain, p. 60
mower, p. 69

nap, p. 18
nibble, p. 21
nickel, p. 72

ocean, p. 60

painter, p. 48
pair, p. 33
panda, p. 66
passport, p. 57
pear, p. 33
peek, p. 21
penny, p. 72
pitcher, p. 36
pitcher, p. 36
playful, p. 48
playground, p. 42
plink, p. 30
polar bear, p. 66
polite, p. 51
pond, p. 60
pounce, p. 21
price, p. 72
puzzled, p. 9

quack, p. 30
quarter, p. 72
quiet, p. 15

rake, p. 69
range, p. 60
rap, p. 33
remake, p. 45
replace, p. 45
reread, p. 45
rest, p. 18
reuse, p. 45
rewrite, p. 45
rhinoceros, p. 66
river, p. 60
rough, p. 27
row, p. 36
row, p. 36
ruler, p. 75
rush, p. 6

sail, p. 33
sale, p. 33
scarecrow, p. 39
scoot, p. 24
scurry, p. 21
sharp, p. 27
shovel, p. 69
show, p. 12
shut, p. 6
sidewalk, p. 42
sign, p. 36
sign, p. 36
simple, p. 9
singer, p. 48
sleepover, p. 57
sleepy, p. 9
sleet, p. 63
slice, p. 6
slimy, p. 27
smile, p. 12
snack, p. 54
sneaky, p. 51
snowflake, p. 42
soar, p. 24
soil, p. 69
spicy, p. 15
spin, p. 18
splash, p. 30
sprinkle, p. 24
squeak, p. 30
stare, p. 21
starfish, p. 39
steal, p. 33
steel, p. 33
stir, p. 18

stream, p. 60
stretch, p. 21
stroll, p. 18
suitcase, p. 57
sunflower, p. 39
surprise, p. 21

take, p. 18
ticket, p. 57
tidal wave, p. 63
tiger, p. 66
tiny, p. 15
toothbrush, p. 39
tornado, p. 63
trace, p. 6
travel, p. 57
turn, p. 18
twist, p. 24

uneven, p. 45
unhappy, p. 45
unpack, p. 45
unsafe, p. 45
untrue, p. 45

vacation, p. 57
visit, p. 57

wallpaper, p. 42
weep, p. 12
wheelchair, p. 39
whisk, p. 18
whisper, p. 12
whole, p. 33
whoosh, p. 30
wiggle, p. 21
wish, p. 6
worm, p. 69
worry, p. 21
wrap, p. 33
wreck, p. 12
wrinkled, p. 27
wristwatch, p. 39
writer, p. 48

yank, p. 24
yard, p. 75
yardstick, p. 75
yell, p. 39

zebra, p. 66

240 Vocabulary Words Kids Need to Know: 2nd Grade © 2012 by Scholastic Inc.

ANSWERS

Lesson 1, page 7: A. 1. glide
2. wish 3. keep 4. shut 5. argue 6. exit
B. 1. slip 2. creep 3. wind 4. face
page 8: Across—4. glide 5. exit
7. choose 9. rush 10. slice; Down—
1. argue 2. wish 3. keep
6. trace 8. shut

Lesson 2, page 10: A. 1. sleepy
2. grumpy 3. breezy 4. bright
5. simple 6. puzzled **B.** 1. coat
2. elephant 3. sponge 4. bed
page 11: 1. hefty 2. cozy 3. sleepy
4. puzzled 5. damp 6. bright
7. grumpy 8. simple 9. breezy
10. icy; Word Search:

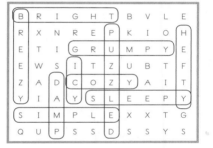

Lesson 3, page 13: A. 1. smile
2. yell 3. frown 4. laugh 5. whisper
6. hide 7. wreck **B.** 1. weep 2. fix
3. show **page 14:** smile/frown;
hide/show; laugh/weep; yell/
whisper; fix/wreck; hidden picture:
elephant

Lesson 4, page 16: A. 1. quiet
2. light 3. spicy 4. early 5. bland
6. late **B.** 1. ant 2. horn 3. castle
4. moon **page 17:** 1. light/dark
2. tiny/huge 3. bland/spicy
4. early/late 5. loud/quiet

Lesson 5, page 19: A. 1. take
2. rest 3. creep 4. grab 5. spin
6. turn **B.** 1. soup 2. eggs 3. park
4. bedroom **page 20:** 1. turn, spin
2. stir, whisk 3. rest, nap 4. take, grab
5. creep, stroll

Lesson 6, page 22: A. 1. peek
2. nibble 3. surprise 4. climb
5. pounce, scurry 6. worry
B. 1. climb 2. run 3. jump 4. sniff
page 23: 1. stare 2. nibble
3. wiggle 4. surprise 5. scurry
6. worry 7. pounce 8. peek 9. climb
10. stretch; Word Search:

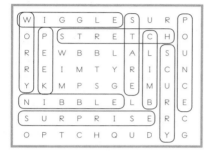

Lesson 7, page 25: A. 1. fasten
2. gaze 3. twist 4. crawl 5. scoot
6. yank **B.** 1. butterfly 2. sky
3. water 4. shirt **page 26:** 1. gaze
2. crawl 3. fasten 4. sprinkle 5. scoot
6. yank 7. twist 8. soar 9. flutter
10. fade; Answer to puzzle: action
word

Lesson 8, page 28: A. 1. furry
2. foamy 3. wrinkled 4. slimy
5. creamy 6. sharp **B.** 1. beach
2. bark 3. cookie 4. gum
page 29: 1. creamy/cake frosting
2. foamy/root beer 3. slimy/worm
4. wrinkled/old person's skin
5. rough/rock 6. gritty/sandpaper
7. chewy/taffy 8. furry/puppy
9. crumbly/cupcake 10. sharp/
scissors

Lesson 9, page 31: A. 1. crackle
2. squeak 3. splash 4. quack
5. chirp 6. ding **B.** 1. umbrella
2. tissue 3. computer mouse
4. car **page 32:** 1. chirp 2. plink
3. splash 4. click 5. crackle 6. quack
7. achoo 8. whoosh 9. squeak
10. ding

Lesson 10, page 34: A. 1. sail
2. hole 3. sale 4. wrap 5. whole
6. pear **B.** 1. two 2. knock 3. take
4. skyscraper **page 35:** 1. Please
water the pear tree. 2. The store
will have a sale on gift wrap in
January. 3. Do not steal the whole
pie! 4. Do you want to sail with me
at the lake? 5. Please rap on the steel
door. 6. I will fix the hole in your pair
of pants tonight.

Lesson 11, page 37: A. 1. row
2. bat 3. ball 4. pitcher, ball 5. sign
6. row **B.** 1. no 2. yes 3. yes
page 38: 1. sign 2. ball 3. bat
4. row 5. sign 6. pitcher 7. row
8. pitcher 9. bat 10. ball

Lesson 12, page 40:
A. 1. wheelchair 2. birdhouse
3. starfish 4. wristwatch 5. firefly
B. 1. tooth + brush 2. drum + stick
3. sun + flower 4. cow + boy
5. scare + crow **page 41:**
1. cowboy 2. drumstick
3. wristwatch 4. sunflower
5. wheelchair 6. toothbrush
7. starfish 8. scarecrow 9. firefly
10. birdhouse

Lesson 13, page 43:
A. 1. sidewalk 2. grasshopper
3. playground 4. snowflake
5. houseboat 6. headphones
B. Order may vary: 1. goldfish
2. greenhouse 3. wallpaper
4. clothespin **page 44:**
1. snowflake 2. goldfish
3. headphones 4. wallpaper
5. clothespin 6. greenhouse
7. playground 8. sidewalk
9. grasshopper 10. houseboat

240 Vocabulary Words Kids Need to Know: 2nd Grade © 2012 by Scholastic Inc.

Lesson 14, page 46: A. 1. reuse
2. reread 3. untrue 4. remake
5. unhappy 6. unsafe **B.** 1. story
2. after a trip 3. broken toy
4. crooked **page 47:** Across—
3. unhappy 4. unsafe 7. reread
8. rewrite; Down—1. remake
2. replace 3. unpack 4. uneven
5. untrue 6. reuse

Lesson 15, page 49: A. 1. joyful
2. colorful 3. careful 4. playful
5. hopeful **B.** 1. writer 2. singer
3. baker 4. painter 5. builder
page 50: 1. singer 2. joyful
3. painter 4. playful 5. baker
6. hopeful 7. careful 8. writer
9. colorful 10. builder; Word Search:

```
I X G B J M H C A R E F U L H
S L A P F U P O R E G U L R W
A P L A Y F U L K E B A K E R
I A O R F D J O Y F U L L T I
S I N G E R A R C L I U R E T
T N R H O P E F U L L D E R E
E T O R F X Y U F U D C X T L
R E T R I Q U L B D E C X T L
I R G B J M H C A M R F U L H
```

Lesson 16, page 52: A. 1. honest
2. gentle 3. bossy 4. polite 5. curious
6. brave **B.** 1. take 2. smile 3. bully
4. tiptoe **page 53:** Good Feelings—
curious, gentle, honest, polite, brave,
friendly; Bad Feelings—bossy,
greedy, mean, sneaky

Lesson 17, page 55:
A. 1. breakfast 2. dinner 3. cafeteria
4. lunch 5. dessert 6. leftovers
B. 1. oven 2. lemonade 3. apple
4. eat food **page 56:** Across—
3. breakfast 4. lunch 5. kitchen
7. dinner 9. dessert; Down—1. drink
2. cafeteria 4. leftovers 6. snack
8. meal

Lesson 18, page 58: A. 1. visit
2. hotel 3. travel 4. vacation
5. camp 6. sleepover **B.** 1. passport
2. ticket 3. map 4. suitcase
page 59: Across—2. sleepover
4. travel 5. camp 7. visit 8. map
9. vacation; Down—1. hotel
3. suitcase 4. ticket 6. passport

Lesson 19, page 61: A. 1. dune
2. cave 3. river 4. range 5. hill
6. pond **B.** 1. river 2. stream 3. ocean
4. lake **page 62:** Land Words—
cave, hill, mountain, dune, range;
Water Words—ocean, river, lake,
pond, stream

Lesson 20, page 64: A.
1. blizzard 2. hail 3. flood
4. dust storm 5. heat wave
B. 1. twilight 2. sunshine 3. clear
4. rain 5. winter **page 65:** Maze—
words in order that they are passed:
dust storm, hail, tidal wave, blizzard,
tornado, heat wave, flood, hurricane,
sleet, fog

Lesson 21, page 67: A. 1. polar
bear 2. elephant 3. camel 4. zebra
5. tiger 6. panda **B.** 1. leopard
2. gorilla 3. rhinoceros 4. giraffe
page 68: 1. elephant 2. tiger
3. polar bear 4. panda 5. camel
6. gorilla 7. zebra 8. rhinoceros
9. leopard 10. giraffe

Lesson 22, page 70: A. 1. worm
2. leaves 3. hose 4. shovel 5. grass,
mower 6. bush **B.** 1. mower
2. grass 3. sun 4. bark **page 71:**
1. leaves 2. worm 3. shovel 4. mower
5. bloom 6. grass 7. hose
8. soil 9. rake 10. bush

Lesson 23, page 73: A. 1. penny
2. nickel 3. dime 4. quarter 5. half-
dollar 6. dollar bill **B.** 1. price
2. cash 3. change 4. coin
page 74: 1. coin 2. dollar bill
3. nickel 4. half-dollar 5. change
6. penny 7. cash 8. dime 9. quarter
10. price; Word Search:

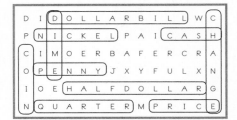

```
D I D O L L A R B I L L W C
P N I C K E L P A I C A S H
C I M O E R B A F E R C R A
O P E N N Y J X Y F U L X N
I O E H A L F D O L L A R G
N Q U A R T E R M P R I C E
```

Lesson 24, page 76: A. 1. yard
2. measure 3. ruler 4. mile
B. 1. meter 2. foot 3. inch
4. centimeter 5. yardstick/meter
stick **page 77:** Units of Measure—
centimeter, mile, foot, meter, inch,
yard; Tools Used to Measure—ruler,
meter stick, yardstick, measure

240 Vocabulary Words Kids Need to Know: 2nd Grade © 2012 by Scholastic Inc.